Tech Titans:

The Untold Stories of Industry Game Changers

By

Karen A. Cox

TABLE OF CONTENTS

Introduction

A. Importance of technology in shaping our world

Technology has become an inseparable part of our lives, permeating every aspect of our society and reshaping the world as we know it. From the moment we wake up to the time we go to bed, we interact with technology in various forms, whether it's through our smartphones, computers, or even the appliances in our homes. The influence of technology extends far beyond mere convenience; it has become a driving force behind the progress and transformation of entire industries, economies, and even governments.

In this rapidly evolving technological landscape, certain individuals have emerged as the trailblazers, the visionaries who have revolutionized their respective industries and left an indelible mark on the world. These individuals, often referred to as tech titans, have wielded their knowledge, innovation, and entrepreneurial spirit to disrupt established norms and usher in a new era of possibilities.

The purpose of this book, "Tech Titans: The Untold Stories of Industry Game Changers," is to delve into the lives and accomplishments of these tech titans and shed light on the untold stories that have shaped the course of technological advancement. While their names might be widely recognized, their personal journeys, motivations, and lesser-known contributions often remain shrouded in mystery.

By exploring these untold stories, we aim to provide a comprehensive understanding of the pivotal role that technology and its champions have played in shaping our world. It is through their unwavering determination, innovative thinking, and transformative ideas that we have witnessed unprecedented progress in fields such as communication, transportation, healthcare, and entertainment.

Moreover, this book seeks to emphasize the importance of technology in addressing the challenges of our time. From tackling climate change to addressing societal inequalities, tech titans have the potential to leverage their resources and expertise for the betterment of humanity. However, the impact of technology goes beyond its potential benefits, as it also raises ethical dilemmas and societal concerns that need to be addressed collectively.

Through an exploration of the untold stories behind these industry game changers, we hope to inspire readers to consider the broader implications of technology and to engage in meaningful discussions about its responsible and sustainable use.

In the following chapters, we will embark on a captivating journey, uncovering the fascinating tales of tech titans, their struggles, triumphs, and the indelible mark they have left on the world. Join us as we unveil the stories that have shaped our present and continue to shape our future, one innovation at a time.

B. The rise of tech titans as influential industry game changers

In the annals of history, there are individuals whose impact transcends their immediate spheres of influence.

They are the visionaries, the innovators, and the disruptors who reshape industries and redefine the boundaries of what is possible. In the realm of technology, these extraordinary individuals are often referred to as tech titans – the game changers who have wielded their intellect, ambition, and relentless pursuit of progress to leave an indelible mark on the world.

The rise of tech titans as influential industry game changers can be traced back to a convergence of factors. Technological advancements, economic shifts, and societal needs have created a fertile ground for these individuals to thrive. They have harnessed the power of emerging technologies and transformed them into tools that revolutionize entire sectors, creating new opportunities, and challenging established norms.

These tech titans have defied the status quo, pushing boundaries and reshaping industries that were once considered impervious to change. Their audacity and entrepreneurial spirit have propelled them from the periphery of the business world to the pinnacle of global influence. Through their unwavering determination, they have disrupted traditional business models, toppled industry giants, and redefined the rules of engagement.

What sets these tech titans apart is not just their ability to innovate, but also their unparalleled vision. They possess an uncanny foresight, an ability to identify nascent trends and seize upon them before they become mainstream. From software and hardware development to artificial intelligence, biotechnology, and beyond, their innovations have redefined how we live, work, and interact with the world around us.

These industry game changers have not only revolutionized specific sectors but have also become synonymous with technological advancement itself. Their names evoke awe and admiration, symbolizing the limitless potential of human ingenuity. From the transformative impact of Steve Jobs and his visionary approach to user-centric design, to the audacious ambitions of Elon Musk, who has disrupted multiple industries with his ventures, tech titans have become household names, inspiring generations to dream big and challenge the status quo.

However, their ascent to the top has not been without its share of controversies and challenges. The influence wielded by tech titans has raised questions about the concentration of power, data privacy, and the ethical implications of their actions. As they continue to push the boundaries of innovation, there is a growing need to examine the social, economic, and political consequences of their dominance.

In "Tech Titans: The Untold Stories of Industry Game Changers," we embark on a journey to uncover the captivating stories behind these influential figures. We will explore their humble beginnings, the obstacles they faced, and the pivotal moments that catapulted them to the forefront of their industries. Through a careful examination of their triumphs and failures, we aim to paint a comprehensive portrait of their journey – one that goes beyond the headlines and reveals the human side of these larger-than-life figures.

Join us as we unravel the stories of the tech titans, explore their motivations, and gain insights into the extraordinary minds that have shaped our technological landscape. Through their stories, we hope to inspire and ignite the spark of innovation within each reader, reminding us that the potential to change the world lies within our reach, waiting to be unlocked through determination, perseverance, and unwavering belief in the power of technology.

C. Overview of the untold stories to be explored in the book

Within the realm of technology, there exists a rich tapestry of untold stories, hidden beneath the surface of well-known narratives. These stories unveil the extraordinary journeys of tech titans, the industry game changers who have shaped our world in profound ways. In this book, "Tech Titans: The Untold Stories of Industry Game Changers," we embark on a captivating exploration of these hidden narratives, shedding light on the lesser-known aspects of their lives and accomplishments.

Prepare to be immersed in a collection of untold stories that offer a fresh perspective on the rise of tech titans and their indelible impact. We delve deep into the annals of history to unearth the pivotal moments, the triumphs, and the setbacks that paved the way for their ascent to greatness. Through meticulous research and interviews with key figures, we bring to the forefront the untold tales that have shaped their extraordinary journeys.

From the visionary brilliance of pioneers such as Ada Lovelace and Alan Turing to the audacious ambitions of contemporary tech titans, we traverse the realms of innovation and discover the stories behind the iconic names. Uncover the fascinating accounts of tech titans who defied conventions and upended established industries, reimagining the very fabric of our lives.

The book showcases the humble beginnings of these industry game changers, revealing the challenges they faced and the unconventional paths they took. These are tales of perseverance, resilience, and the relentless pursuit of their visions. We delve into the garages and dorm rooms where revolutionary ideas were born, examining the struggles and sacrifices that laid the foundation for their meteoric rise.

But our exploration does not end with the initial breakthroughs. We venture into the domains of disruptive technologies and industries, witnessing firsthand the seismic shifts brought about by these tech titans. Peek behind the curtains of their most celebrated achievements and uncover the hidden stories of collaboration, competition, and the quest for dominance.

The book also delves into the ethical dilemmas and societal impact engendered by their immense influence. We confront the controversies that have surrounded their actions, exploring the delicate balance between progress and responsibility. By illuminating these nuanced discussions, we invite readers to critically reflect on the consequences of unchecked power and the need for ethical considerations in our rapidly evolving technological landscape.

Moreover, "Tech Titans: The Untold Stories of Industry Game Changers" takes you beyond the boardrooms and corporate endeavors. Discover the personal lives, motivations, and philanthropic endeavors of these titans. Gain insights into their human side, exploring the passions that drive their pursuits and the legacies they strive to leave behind.

As we conclude this captivating journey, we cast our gaze towards the future. Speculate with us on the upcoming innovations, as we ponder the potential pathways these tech titans will traverse. Reflect on the enduring legacies they have created and the profound impact they will continue to have on our lives and the generations to come.

Join us on this compelling expedition as we peel back the layers of history and present the untold stories of tech titans – the exceptional individuals who have reshaped industries, inspired innovation, and left an indelible mark on the world. Brace yourself for a thought-provoking, awe-inspiring experience that will deepen your understanding of the tech titans' remarkable contributions and ignite your own spirit of curiosity and possibility.

Chapter 1
Visionaries of the Digital Age

A. Early pioneers and their groundbreaking ideas

The advent of the digital age was made possible by the visionary thinkers and early pioneers who dared to imagine a world transformed by technology. In this chapter, we delve into the lives and ideas of these trailblazers who laid the foundation for the tech titans that would later emerge.

We begin by peering into the origins of computing and the brilliant minds that propelled it forward. From the mathematical genius of Charles Babbage, who conceived the concept of a programmable computing machine in the 19th century, to the pioneering work of Ada Lovelace, often credited as the world's first computer programmer, we uncover the early sparks of innovation that set the stage for the digital revolution.

As we venture further into the 20th century, we encounter the groundbreaking ideas that shaped the trajectory of technology. We explore the brilliant mind of

Alan Turing, whose groundbreaking work in cryptography and computer science paved the way for modern computing. Turing's visionary concepts, such as the Turing Machine and the notion of artificial intelligence, laid the groundwork for the future advancements that would shape our world.

Moving beyond the realm of theory, we delve into the stories of inventors and entrepreneurs who transformed these ideas into reality. One such pioneer is Douglas Engelbart, whose invention of the computer mouse and the concept of interactive computing revolutionized the way we interact with computers. His groundbreaking ideas and relentless pursuit of innovation propelled the world into the era of user-friendly computing.

We also examine the contributions of Xerox PARC (Palo Alto Research Center), a legendary research facility that gave birth to numerous groundbreaking inventions. From the development of the graphical user interface (GUI) to the creation of Ethernet and laser printing, the visionary researchers at Xerox PARC forged the path for the future of computing and set the stage for the emergence of tech titans.

Throughout this chapter, we aim to shed light on the often overlooked stories of these early pioneers and their groundbreaking ideas. Their intellectual curiosity, audacity, and unwavering belief in the potential of technology laid the groundwork for the transformative innovations we enjoy today. By delving into their journeys and understanding the challenges they faced, we gain a deeper appreciation for their contributions and the profound impact they have had on shaping the digital age.

Join us as we explore the world of visionaries who laid the groundwork for the rise of tech titans. Be inspired by their intellectual brilliance, their daring ideas, and their unwavering commitment to pushing the boundaries of what was possible. Their groundbreaking contributions form the bedrock upon which the tech titans would build, and their stories deserve to be celebrated and remembered as we navigate the ever-evolving landscape of technology.

B. Profiles of key tech titans and their impact

In this chapter, we delve into the lives and legacies of key tech titans who have left an indelible mark on the digital age. Through their groundbreaking innovations and visionary leadership, these individuals have transformed industries, shaped our technological landscape, and influenced the way we live, work, and connect.

One of the towering figures we examine is Steve Jobs, the co-founder of Apple Inc. With his relentless pursuit of perfection and an unwavering commitment to user-friendly design, Jobs revolutionized the personal computing industry. From the introduction of the Macintosh to the creation of iconic products such as the iPod, iPhone, and iPad, Jobs' ability to anticipate consumer needs and deliver revolutionary devices cemented Apple's position as a global tech powerhouse.

Another tech titan we explore is Bill Gates, the co-founder of Microsoft Corporation. Gates played a pivotal role in bringing computers to the masses with the development of the Windows operating system. His vision of a computer on every desk and in every home became a reality, reshaping the way we work, communicate, and access information. Gates' philanthropic efforts through the Bill & Melinda Gates Foundation have also made a significant impact on global health, education, and poverty alleviation.

We also shine a spotlight on Mark Zuckerberg, the co-founder of Facebook, a platform that redefined social networking and how we connect with others. From its humble origins as a college dorm project, Facebook grew into a global phenomenon, with billions of users worldwide. Zuckerberg's bold vision to create a connected world has had far-reaching implications, influencing not only social interactions but also shaping the digital advertising landscape.

Additionally, we examine the remarkable impact of Elon Musk, the visionary entrepreneur behind companies like Tesla, SpaceX, and Neuralink. Musk's audacious goals, from revolutionizing the electric vehicle industry to making space travel accessible, have pushed the boundaries of what was once deemed possible. His vision of sustainable energy and interplanetary exploration has garnered global attention and galvanized industries to reimagine what the future holds.

Through these profiles and more, we aim to offer readers a deeper understanding of the tech titans who have shaped the digital age. We explore their motivations, their personal journeys, and the impact their companies and innovations have had on society, economy, and technology. Their bold visions, unwavering determination, and willingness to challenge conventions have not only transformed industries but have also inspired a new generation of entrepreneurs and innovators.

As we delve into these profiles, we also recognize the controversies and challenges that have accompanied the rise of these tech titans. We critically examine the ethical implications of their actions, the debates surrounding data privacy, and the concentration of power within these dominant companies. By presenting a comprehensive view of their impact, we encourage readers to engage in thoughtful discussions about the responsibility and societal implications of influential industry game changers.

Join us as we embark on a journey through the lives of key tech titans, exploring their visionary ideas, disruptive innovations, and the enduring impact they have had on our digital world. Through their stories, we gain insights into the transformative power of human imagination and the potential for technology to shape the course of history.

C. Uncovering lesser-known stories and contributions

In this chapter, we embark on a fascinating journey of uncovering the lesser-known stories and contributions of the visionaries who shaped the digital age. While their names may not be as widely recognized as some of their contemporaries, their ideas and innovations have had a profound impact on our technological landscape.

We delve into the life and work of Grace Hopper, a pioneer in computer programming and a trailblazer for women in technology. Hopper's groundbreaking contributions include the development of the first compiler and the programming language COBOL. Her relentless dedication to advancing computer science and her advocacy for diversity in the field have paved the way for future generations of female technologists.

Another unsung hero we explore is Tim Berners-Lee, the inventor of the World Wide Web. Berners-Lee's visionary idea to create a global system for sharing information revolutionized communication and laid the foundation for the internet as we know it today. His commitment to an open and accessible web has shaped the digital landscape, empowering individuals around the world to connect, collaborate, and share knowledge.

We also shine a light on the contributions of Radia Perlman, often referred to as the "Mother of the Internet." Perlman's work on the spanning-tree protocol was instrumental in the development of modern computer networks. Her innovative approach to network routing has enabled the seamless transmission of data across vast distances, playing a crucial role in the scalability and reliability of the internet.

Additionally, we uncover the lesser-known story of Robert Noyce, a co-founder of Intel Corporation and one of the pioneers of the microchip. Noyce's groundbreaking work in developing the integrated circuit paved the way for the miniaturization of electronics and the birth of the modern semiconductor industry. His vision and leadership have left an enduring legacy in the world of computing.

Through these and other captivating stories, we aim to shed light on the hidden contributions of these unsung heroes who played a crucial role in shaping the digital age. Their innovative ideas, perseverance, and commitment to advancing technology have often gone unnoticed in the broader narrative, but their impact cannot be underestimated.

By delving into these lesser-known stories, we provide a more comprehensive view of the digital revolution, showcasing the diverse range of minds and contributions that have shaped our technological landscape. Their innovations have touched countless lives, transforming industries, and laying the groundwork for the tech titans that would emerge in the years to come.

Join us as we uncover the remarkable stories and unsung contributions of these visionaries of the digital age. Through their lesser-known narratives, we gain a deeper appreciation for the depth and breadth of human ingenuity and the countless threads that intertwine to create the tapestry of technological progress.

Chapter 2
From Garages to Global Dominance

A. Examining the humble beginnings of tech giants

In this chapter, we embark on a captivating exploration of the humble beginnings of tech giants, tracing their journeys from modest origins to the pinnacle of global dominance. From garages, dorm rooms, and small offices, these industry game changers started their remarkable ascent with nothing more than a spark of innovation, unwavering determination, and a vision for the future.

We delve into the early days of Microsoft, where Bill Gates and Paul Allen transformed their passion for computers into a business that would revolutionize the software industry. In the nondescript Albuquerque motel room where Gates and Allen famously signed their first major deal, the seeds of a tech empire were sown. We unravel the story of their perseverance, late-night coding sessions, and the audacity to dream big.

Another captivating tale we explore is that of Apple Inc., born in the legendary garage of Steve Jobs' childhood home. This unassuming space witnessed the birth of the Apple I, the first step towards a company that would redefine personal computing. We delve into the hardships faced by Jobs, Steve Wozniak, and Ronald Wayne as they poured their hearts and minds into their revolutionary creations, ultimately birthing the company that would become a global icon.

We also shine a light on Amazon's origins, tracing its roots back to Jeff Bezos' humble office in his garage. The visionary entrepreneur's relentless pursuit of his e-commerce dream would lead to the creation of an online marketplace that would forever change the retail landscape. We explore the challenges faced by Bezos in the early days, from packing books in his car to navigating the turbulent waters of the dot-com bubble.

Furthermore, we delve into the humble beginnings of Google, which sprouted from the Stanford University dorm rooms of Larry Page and Sergey Brin. Armed with a powerful search algorithm and a commitment to organizing the world's information, they transformed their university project into the world's most widely used search engine. We unravel the story of their friendship, their relentless pursuit of innovation, and the leap of faith that led to the birth of a tech behemoth.

Through these and other compelling narratives, we aim to provide a glimpse into the early struggles, setbacks, and pivotal moments that shaped these tech giants. We celebrate the entrepreneurial spirit, resourcefulness, and resilience that propelled them forward in the face of adversity. From humble beginnings to global dominance, their stories remind us that greatness can emerge from even the most unlikely of places.

Join us as we journey back to the garages, dorm rooms, and small offices where the seeds of tech giants were sown. Discover the stories of triumph and tenacity, of risk-taking and perseverance. By examining their humble beginnings, we gain a deeper appreciation for the transformative power of ideas, passion, and unwavering determination. These tales of ascent inspire us to nurture our own sparks of innovation, reminding us that the journey from humble origins to global dominance is one that can be embarked upon by anyone with a dream and the courage to pursue it.

B. The challenges and obstacles faced during their rise

The path from garages to global dominance is rarely smooth for tech giants. In this chapter, we delve into the challenges and obstacles that these industry game changers encountered on their journey to the top. From financial constraints to technological barriers and fierce competition, their rise to prominence was marked by numerous trials and tribulations.

One of the recurring challenges faced by tech giants was securing funding and overcoming financial hurdles. We explore how founders like Bill Gates and Paul Allen struggled to convince investors of the viability of their ideas in the early days of Microsoft. These budding entrepreneurs faced countless rejections and had to scrape together resources to turn their visions into reality.

Technological barriers also posed significant obstacles along the way. Steve Jobs and his team at Apple encountered numerous technical challenges in developing their revolutionary products. From engineering hurdles to software glitches, the pursuit of perfection often meant overcoming seemingly insurmountable technological barriers.

In addition, fierce competition emerged as a constant threat to the rise of tech giants. We delve into the fierce battles between companies like Apple and Microsoft, as well as the intense rivalry between Google and other search engine contenders. These titans had to navigate legal disputes, market competition, and shifting consumer preferences to solidify their positions in the industry.

Furthermore, scaling operations to meet growing demand presented its own set of challenges. Jeff Bezos and Amazon faced logistical hurdles in building a robust supply chain and establishing a global infrastructure. The need to expand rapidly while maintaining quality and efficiency required innovative solutions and relentless determination.

Moreover, the evolving regulatory landscape posed significant challenges for these tech giants. As their influence grew, they faced increased scrutiny from governments and regulatory bodies. We explore the legal battles, antitrust investigations, and public controversies that these companies encountered as they grappled with navigating complex regulatory environments.

Throughout this chapter, we aim to showcase the resilience and tenacity of these tech giants in overcoming the challenges that stood in their way. Despite the odds, they persisted, adapting their strategies, learning from failures, and forging new paths forward. Their ability to innovate, pivot, and embrace change played a crucial role in their eventual ascent to global dominance.

Join us as we uncover the challenges and obstacles faced by these industry game changers on their rise to prominence. Through their stories, we gain insights into the determination, resourcefulness, and strategic thinking required to overcome adversity. These tales of resilience remind us that success is rarely linear, but rather a result of perseverance and the ability to turn obstacles into opportunities.

C. Strategies and innovations that propelled them to success

In this chapter, we delve into the strategies and innovations that propelled tech giants from their humble beginnings to the heights of global dominance. These industry game changers employed visionary tactics, disruptive innovations, and bold moves to carve their path to success.

One key strategy embraced by tech giants was a relentless focus on innovation. Companies like Apple, Microsoft, and Google set themselves apart by introducing groundbreaking products and services that revolutionized their respective industries. They fostered cultures of creativity and encouraged their teams to think outside the box, resulting in a continuous stream of game-changing innovations.

A pivotal strategy employed by these giants was their ability to anticipate and capitalize on emerging trends. They possessed an uncanny knack for identifying market gaps and consumer needs before they became mainstream. Whether it was Apple's foresight in recognizing the demand for sleek, user-friendly devices, or Google's realization that organizing the world's information was the key to online search dominance, these companies were able to stay ahead of the curve.

Tech giants also leveraged strategic partnerships and acquisitions to bolster their growth. Collaborations with complementary businesses, such as Microsoft's partnership with IBM in the early days, enabled them to tap into existing networks and expand their reach. Additionally, strategic acquisitions allowed these companies to access new technologies, talent, and customer bases, propelling their growth and further solidifying their dominance.

Another hallmark of their success was a relentless focus on user experience. These tech giants recognized that a seamless, intuitive user interface could be a differentiating factor in a crowded market. Companies like Apple and Google prioritized user-centric design, creating products and services that were not only functional but also aesthetically pleasing and easy to use. This commitment to user experience fostered loyalty and helped drive their success.

Furthermore, these industry game changers embraced a culture of continuous improvement. They were not afraid to iterate and refine their products and services based on user feedback and evolving market demands. This iterative approach allowed them to stay agile and responsive, adapting to changing customer needs and market dynamics.

Lastly, the ability to envision and create ecosystems around their products and services played a crucial role in their success. Tech giants like Amazon and Apple built vast ecosystems that encompassed hardware, software, content, and services. By offering an integrated and seamless experience to users, they created strong customer loyalty and lock-in, solidifying their position as dominant players in their respective industries.

Join us as we delve into the strategies and innovations that propelled these industry game changers to global dominance. From a relentless focus on innovation and anticipating emerging trends to strategic partnerships, user-centric design, and the creation of powerful ecosystems, these companies employed a multifaceted approach that paved the way for their success. Through their stories, we gain insights into the strategies that can be applied to our own endeavors, reminding us that with vision, innovation, and strategic thinking, we too can chart a course towards greatness.

Chapter 3
Disruptive Technologies and Industries

A. Exploration of transformative technologies introduced by tech titans

In this chapter, we embark on an exploration of the transformative technologies introduced by tech titans, technologies that have disrupted industries, reshaped the way we live and work, and propelled these industry game changers to the forefront of innovation.

One of the transformative technologies we delve into is the smartphone revolution ignited by Apple's iPhone. This sleek, touchscreen device revolutionized the way we communicate, consume media, and access information. Its introduction heralded a new era of mobile computing, creating a platform for countless applications and paving the way for a connected world at our fingertips.

We also explore the revolutionary impact of cloud computing, a technology pioneered by Amazon Web Services (AWS). The ability to store and access data and applications remotely, on-demand, and at scale revolutionized the way businesses operate. The advent of cloud computing empowered companies of all sizes to leverage the power of scalable infrastructure, transforming industries and enabling new business models.

The rise of e-commerce, spearheaded by companies like Amazon, reshaped the retail landscape. We examine how online shopping and digital marketplaces disrupted traditional brick-and-mortar retail, providing consumers with convenience, choice, and competitive pricing. These e-commerce platforms created new opportunities for businesses and opened up global markets, transforming the way we buy and sell goods.

Moreover, we explore the transformative impact of artificial intelligence (AI) and machine learning. Tech titans like Google and Microsoft have leveraged AI to develop intelligent algorithms, natural language processing, and computer vision capabilities. These advancements have revolutionized fields such as search engines, digital assistants, and autonomous vehicles, pushing the boundaries of what machines can accomplish.

Additionally, we delve into the transformative power of streaming services and digital content distribution. Companies like Netflix and Spotify disrupted traditional media and entertainment industries, revolutionizing the way we consume movies, TV shows, and music. These platforms introduced on-demand access to a vast library of content, challenging established distribution models and giving rise to a new era of personalized entertainment.

Through exploring these transformative technologies, we gain a deeper understanding of the immense impact they have had on society, economy, and culture. These technologies have not only disrupted industries but have also reshaped consumer behavior, redefined business models, and opened up new possibilities for innovation and collaboration.

Join us as we delve into the transformative technologies introduced by tech titans, unveiling the stories behind their creation and the impact they have had on our world. Through their innovations, these industry game changers have propelled us into a new era, where connectivity, efficiency, and limitless possibilities are the norm.

B. Disruption of traditional industries and the resulting impact

In this chapter, we delve into the profound disruption caused by tech titans in traditional industries, and the consequential impact on various sectors of the economy. The relentless pursuit of innovation and the introduction of transformative technologies by these industry game changers have reshaped long-established industries, challenging traditional business models and forever altering the way we live and work.

One sector that has experienced significant disruption is the retail industry, which has been profoundly transformed by the rise of e-commerce giants such as Amazon. Traditional brick-and-mortar retailers have struggled to compete with the convenience, choice, and competitive pricing offered by online shopping platforms. The advent of digital marketplaces has not only revolutionized the way we shop but has also prompted traditional retailers to reevaluate their strategies and adapt to the new digital landscape.

The entertainment industry has also undergone a seismic shift due to the disruptive technologies introduced by tech titans. Streaming services like Netflix and platforms like YouTube have challenged the dominance of traditional media outlets. These digital platforms have democratized content creation and distribution, allowing independent creators to reach global audiences directly. As a result, traditional broadcasting and distribution models have been upended, leading to a paradigm shift in how we consume movies, TV shows, and music.

The transportation industry has also been disrupted by tech titans like Uber and Lyft, who introduced the concept of ride-hailing services. These companies have revolutionized urban mobility, offering convenient, affordable, and on-demand transportation options. The rise of ride-sharing has not only transformed the way we commute but has also sparked debates around regulations, labor practices, and the future of transportation.

Additionally, the financial sector has experienced significant disruption through the introduction of fintech innovations. Companies like PayPal, Square, and Stripe have revolutionized online payments, making transactions more secure, convenient, and efficient. Peer-to-peer lending platforms and digital banking services have also challenged traditional financial institutions, forcing them to adapt and innovate in order to remain competitive.

Furthermore, the healthcare industry has been impacted by the introduction of digital health technologies and telemedicine services. Tech titans have leveraged advancements in artificial intelligence, wearable devices, and remote patient monitoring to improve healthcare access, enhance diagnostics, and transform patient care. The integration of technology into healthcare has opened up new possibilities for personalized medicine, patient empowerment, and cost-effective healthcare delivery.

Through exploring these disruptions, we gain insights into the far-reaching impact of tech titans on traditional industries. The disruption of established sectors has spurred innovation, increased efficiency, and empowered consumers with greater choice and convenience. However, these transformations have also raised questions about regulation, privacy, job displacement, and societal implications, prompting ongoing discussions and debates.

Join us as we delve into the disruptive technologies introduced by tech titans and the resulting impact on traditional industries. Through their innovations, these industry game changers have reshaped the economy, challenged the status quo, and ushered in an era of unprecedented change. By examining the transformative power of their disruptions, we gain a deeper understanding of the complex dynamics between technology, industries, and society at large.

C. Unveiling the behind-the-scenes battles and triumphs

In this chapter, we peel back the curtain and delve into the behind-the-scenes battles and triumphs of tech titans as they disrupted industries with their transformative technologies. While the world marveled at their successes, the journey to global dominance was fraught with intense competition, strategic maneuvering, and hard-fought victories.

We explore the behind-the-scenes battles that took place as these industry game changers faced formidable opponents. In the early days, tech titans like Microsoft waged fierce battles against established giants, including IBM, in the quest for market dominance. We uncover the strategies employed, the partnerships forged, and the innovation race that unfolded as these companies vied for supremacy.

Additionally, we examine the legal and regulatory battles that accompanied their rise to dominance. Tech giants found themselves entangled in antitrust investigations, intellectual property disputes, and privacy controversies. We shine a light on the courtroom dramas and regulatory challenges that shaped the tech landscape, exploring how these industry leaders navigated the legal complexities while continuing to disrupt and innovate.

Beyond the legal arena, we uncover the behind-the-scenes triumphs that propelled these tech titans forward. We explore the moments of breakthrough and innovation that allowed them to leap ahead of the competition. From groundbreaking product launches that captivated the world to strategic acquisitions that bolstered their capabilities, we unveil the pivotal triumphs that solidified their position at the top.

Moreover, we delve into the strategic maneuvers and business negotiations that shaped the trajectories of these industry game changers. From partnerships and alliances to strategic investments and mergers, we uncover the pivotal deals that reshaped entire industries. These strategic moves allowed tech titans to expand their reach, acquire talent and technology, and strengthen their competitive edge.

Throughout these battles and triumphs, we witness the resilience, determination, and strategic thinking that propelled tech titans to the forefront of innovation. These behind-the-scenes stories reveal the intense pressure, calculated risks, and pivotal moments that defined their journeys. They showcase the visionary leadership, the relentless pursuit of excellence, and the unwavering belief in their mission that allowed them to overcome challenges and emerge triumphant.

Join us as we unveil the behind-the-scenes battles and triumphs of tech titans, providing a glimpse into the high-stakes world of disruptive technologies and industries. Through these stories, we gain a deeper appreciation for the strategic acumen, the innovation prowess, and the relentless drive that propelled these industry game changers to global dominance. By understanding the battles they fought and the triumphs they achieved, we gain insights into the intricate dynamics of innovation, competition, and strategic maneuvering that continue to shape our rapidly evolving technological landscape.

Chapter 4
Ethical Dilemmas and Societal Impact

A. The ethical considerations surrounding tech titan practices

In this chapter, we delve into the ethical dilemmas and societal impact engendered by the practices of tech titans. While these industry game changers have transformed our world with their innovations, their immense power and influence have raised important ethical considerations that demand our attention and reflection.

One key area of ethical concern is data privacy. Tech titans collect vast amounts of user data, raising questions about how that data is used, stored, and protected. We examine the controversies surrounding data breaches, unauthorized data sharing, and the monetization of personal information. The impact of these practices on individuals' privacy and autonomy is a critical ethical consideration in our increasingly connected world.

Furthermore, we explore the potential implications of artificial intelligence (AI) and machine learning. The use of AI algorithms to make decisions that affect individuals, such as in hiring processes or criminal justice systems, raises concerns about bias, fairness, and accountability. We delve into the ethical considerations surrounding algorithmic transparency, the responsible deployment of AI, and the potential consequences of automated decision-making.

The concentration of power in the hands of tech titans is another ethical concern. We examine the implications of their dominant market positions and the potential for anticompetitive behavior. The practices of acquiring potential competitors, stifling innovation through exclusivity agreements, and leveraging data advantages raise questions about fairness, market competition, and consumer choice.

Additionally, we explore the ethical considerations surrounding the impact of technology on labor markets. Automation and artificial intelligence have the potential to displace jobs and reshape entire industries. We examine the ethical responsibility of tech titans in ensuring a just transition for workers, addressing the societal implications of technological unemployment, and fostering inclusive growth in the face of rapid technological advancements.

Moreover, we delve into the ethical dilemmas surrounding content moderation and the spread of misinformation on digital platforms. Tech titans have grappled with the challenge of balancing free speech, protecting users from harmful content, and preventing the dissemination of false information. We explore the challenges they face in maintaining a healthy online environment while respecting the principles of free expression and avoiding undue censorship.

Through examining these ethical considerations, we aim to foster a critical dialogue about the responsible use of technology and the societal impact of tech titans. We invite readers to reflect on the potential consequences of unchecked power and the need for ethical guidelines in the development and deployment of technologies. These considerations prompt us to contemplate the values we uphold as a society and the measures we can take to ensure technology is harnessed for the greater good.

Join us as we navigate the complex landscape of ethical dilemmas surrounding tech titan practices. By critically examining these issues, we deepen our understanding of the ethical dimensions of technological advancements and the importance of ensuring that innovation is accompanied by responsible, ethically informed decision-making.

B. Examination of controversies and their consequences

In this chapter, we undertake a comprehensive examination of the controversies surrounding tech titans and the far-reaching consequences of these ethical dilemmas. As industry game changers, these companies have faced significant scrutiny and criticism for their practices, leading to profound societal repercussions and a reevaluation of the role and responsibilities of tech titans.

One major controversy we explore is the Cambridge Analytica scandal, which rocked Facebook and ignited a global conversation about data privacy and the misuse of personal information. The revelation that millions of Facebook users' data had been harvested without their consent for political purposes raised serious ethical concerns. We analyze the consequences of this controversy, including increased scrutiny on data privacy regulations, a loss of trust in social media platforms, and a call for greater transparency and accountability.

Additionally, we delve into the controversies surrounding content moderation on digital platforms. From the spread of misinformation and hate speech to the challenges of striking the right balance between free expression and harmful content, tech titans have faced intense public scrutiny. We examine the consequences of these controversies, including calls for stricter regulations, demands for greater transparency in content moderation policies, and debates around the power and responsibility of tech companies in shaping public discourse.

Furthermore, we explore controversies surrounding labor practices within the tech industry. Issues such as worker exploitation, inadequate diversity and inclusion, and unfair treatment of gig economy workers have drawn attention to the social and ethical implications of tech titan practices. We examine the consequences of these controversies, including demands for better working conditions, calls for equitable representation, and a broader discourse on the ethical responsibilities of tech companies toward their employees.

The consequences of these controversies extend beyond individual companies and have prompted wider societal discussions. They have led to increased public awareness about the potential risks and unintended consequences of technological advancements. As a result, there has been a growing demand for stronger regulations, increased accountability, and a more comprehensive examination of the societal impact of tech titans.

Through examining these controversies and their consequences, we aim to foster a nuanced understanding of the ethical dilemmas inherent in the practices of tech titans. These controversies have prompted important conversations about privacy, free speech, labor rights, and the power dynamics in the digital age. By shedding light on these issues, we encourage readers to critically engage with the implications of tech titan actions and advocate for ethical practices and responsible innovation.

Join us as we navigate the intricate landscape of controversies surrounding tech titans and their far-reaching consequences. By examining these controversies, we gain insights into the profound impact of their practices on individuals, society, and the wider technological ecosystem. Through thoughtful examination and discourse, we can strive for ethical guidelines and responsible practices that ensure the benefits of technology are balanced with the protection of fundamental rights and societal well-being.

C. Evaluating the societal impact and the need for regulation

In this chapter, we undertake a comprehensive evaluation of the societal impact of tech titans and the growing need for regulation in the face of ethical dilemmas. As these industry game changers continue to shape our world, it is essential to critically examine the consequences of their actions and assess the necessity for regulatory measures to ensure a responsible and equitable technological landscape.

We begin by assessing the societal impact of tech titans' practices. While their innovations have undoubtedly brought numerous benefits and advancements, we must also acknowledge the potential negative consequences. We delve into the issues of increasing economic inequality, the displacement of traditional industries, and the potential erosion of privacy rights. By critically evaluating these impacts, we gain a deeper understanding of the complex dynamics between technological progress and societal well-being.

Furthermore, we explore the power dynamics inherent in the operations of tech titans and the implications for democracy and civic discourse. The influence these companies wield over information dissemination, content moderation, and algorithmic decision-making raises concerns about potential biases, filter bubbles, and the manipulation of public opinion. We analyze the impact on democratic processes and the need for transparency and accountability in shaping the digital public sphere.

As we assess the societal impact, it becomes evident that the need for regulatory intervention is increasingly urgent. We examine the limitations of self-regulation and the importance of comprehensive legal frameworks to safeguard individual rights and societal values. We explore the role of governments and regulatory bodies in setting guidelines and enforcing standards to address the ethical dilemmas posed by tech titans.

Additionally, we delve into the importance of fostering responsible innovation through regulatory measures. Striking the right balance between innovation and ethical considerations is crucial to ensure that technology serves the broader interests of society. We analyze the need for regulations that promote data privacy, protect consumer rights, and prevent anti competitive practices. By establishing clear rules and boundaries, we can mitigate the potential harms associated with unchecked technological advancements.

Moreover, we explore the importance of international cooperation in regulating tech titans. As these companies operate on a global scale, a coordinated effort among nations is crucial to address the ethical dilemmas and societal impact. We examine the challenges and potential frameworks for global collaboration to ensure a harmonized approach to regulation that transcends national boundaries.

Through evaluating the societal impact and the need for regulation, we aim to foster a thoughtful dialogue about the future of technology and its ethical implications. It is essential that we collectively address the challenges posed by tech titans and work towards a technological landscape that prioritizes the well-being and values of individuals and society as a whole.

Join us as we critically evaluate the societal impact of tech titans and navigate the complexities of regulation in the digital age. By acknowledging the ethical dilemmas and advocating for responsible practices, we can shape a future where technology and innovation align with the greater good, ensuring a fair, inclusive, and sustainable technological landscape.

Chapter 5
Collaboration and Competition

A. Interactions and partnerships among tech titans

In this chapter, we delve into the intricate web of interactions and partnerships that have emerged among tech titans. While these industry game changers are known for their fierce competition, they have also engaged in collaborations and strategic alliances that have shaped the technological landscape in profound ways.

We explore the strategic partnerships that have formed between tech titans to drive innovation and create synergies. For instance, we examine the collaboration between Apple and Google, where Google's search engine became the default option on Apple's Safari browser, leading to a mutually beneficial relationship that elevated both companies' prominence. We analyze the motivations, benefits, and impact of such partnerships on the broader ecosystem.

Furthermore, we delve into the cooperative efforts in standardization and industry consortia that have brought tech titans together. The development of open standards, such as HTML and TCP/IP, have facilitated interoperability and the growth of the internet. We explore the dynamics of these collaborative initiatives and the role they play in fostering innovation, driving industry-wide progress, and ensuring compatibility across platforms.

We also examine the acquisitions and mergers that have reshaped the tech landscape. Tech titans have strategically acquired smaller companies to gain access to valuable technologies, talent, and intellectual property. We explore high-profile acquisitions, such as Facebook's acquisition of Instagram and WhatsApp, and Google's acquisition of YouTube, assessing the impact of these mergers on the companies involved, as well as the broader competitive landscape.

Additionally, we delve into the competitive dynamics among tech titans, analyzing their battles for market share, technological supremacy, and customer loyalty. We explore the intense rivalry between companies like

Apple and Samsung in the smartphone market, Amazon and Walmart in e-commerce, and Google and Microsoft in search and productivity tools. We examine the strategies employed, the innovative breakthroughs, and the repercussions of these fierce competitions.

Through an exploration of both collaborations and competitions, we gain insights into the complex interplay between cooperation and rivalry in the tech industry. These interactions and partnerships showcase the dynamic nature of the sector, where companies simultaneously collaborate to drive progress and compete to secure their positions.

Join us as we unravel the intricate tapestry of interactions and partnerships among tech titans. By examining the collaborations, mergers, and rivalries that have defined the industry, we gain a deeper understanding of the forces at play and the dynamics that shape the technological landscape. These stories of collaboration and competition highlight the remarkable resilience, adaptability, and strategic thinking that have propelled tech titans to their positions of influence and reshaped our world.

B. Rivalries and competitive strategies shaping the industry

In this chapter, we delve into the intense rivalries and competitive strategies that have shaped the tech industry, driving innovation, challenging the status quo, and ultimately transforming the way we live and work. These rivalries between tech titans have been at the forefront of industry dynamics, fueling technological advancements and pushing the boundaries of what is possible.

One of the most iconic rivalries in the tech world is the battle between Apple and Microsoft. We explore how these two giants competed fiercely in the personal computing market, each striving for dominance. From the early days of the Macintosh versus Windows to the evolution of iOS and Windows Phone, their competition spurred innovation, user-centric design, and the continuous improvement of operating systems.

Another notable rivalry is between Google and Microsoft, particularly in the realm of search and productivity tools. We examine the battle for search engine supremacy, with Google's emergence as the dominant player and Microsoft's subsequent efforts to challenge its dominance with Bing. We also explore the competition in productivity suites, with Google's G Suite and Microsoft's Office 365 vying for the loyalty of businesses and individuals.

In the e-commerce sector, the rivalry between Amazon and traditional retailers like Walmart has reshaped the retail landscape. We delve into the fierce competition for market share, the race to offer convenient and fast delivery options, and the battle for dominance in online retail. This rivalry has fueled innovation in logistics, supply chain management, and customer experience, resulting in significant shifts in consumer behavior and expectations.

Furthermore, we explore the rivalry between Tesla and traditional automotive manufacturers in the electric vehicle (EV) market. Tesla's disruptive approach to EVs challenged established players, forcing them to accelerate their own electric vehicle development and redefine their strategies. We analyze how this competition has spurred advancements in battery technology, charging infrastructure, and autonomous driving, driving the transition to a more sustainable transportation future.

Additionally, we delve into the rivalry between social media giants Facebook and Twitter. We examine their competition for user engagement, advertising revenue, and influence in shaping public discourse. We analyze their different approaches to content moderation, algorithmic feed customization, and the challenges they face in addressing issues of misinformation, hate speech, and user privacy.

Through exploring these rivalries and competitive strategies, we gain insights into the dynamics that have propelled the tech industry forward. These rivalries have resulted in groundbreaking innovations, enhanced user experiences, and a continuous push for improvement. They have challenged traditional norms, disrupted established markets, and fueled the constant drive for innovation and market leadership.

Join us as we uncover the rivalries and competitive strategies that have shaped the tech industry. By examining these dynamics, we gain a deeper understanding of the fierce competition, strategic maneuvering, and relentless pursuit of excellence that have driven tech titans to innovate and transform our world. These stories of rivalries and competitive strategies showcase the resilience, determination, and ingenuity that define the industry and have led to the technological advancements we enjoy today.

C. Insights into unexpected collaborations and their outcomes

In this chapter, we explore the fascinating realm of unexpected collaborations among tech titans, uncovering the surprising alliances that have emerged and the outcomes that have shaped the industry. These collaborations, often unexpected in nature, have resulted in unique synergies, innovative breakthroughs, and transformative impacts on the tech landscape.

One notable example of an unexpected collaboration is the partnership between Apple and Intel. Historically, Apple relied on PowerPC processors for its Mac computers. However, in a surprising move, Apple announced a transition to Intel processors in 2005. This collaboration allowed Apple to leverage Intel's technological expertise, resulting in improved performance, greater energy efficiency, and enhanced compatibility with mainstream software. The outcome was a significant boost to Apple's market position and a shift that ultimately redefined the Mac line of products.

Another unexpected collaboration is the partnership between IBM and Apple in the enterprise sector. IBM, traditionally known for its enterprise software and services, joined forces with Apple to develop business-focused applications for iOS devices. This collaboration brought together Apple's user-friendly hardware and interface design with IBM's deep industry knowledge and enterprise capabilities. The outcome was a series of powerful enterprise apps, such as IBM MobileFirst, that transformed the way businesses leverage mobile technology for improved productivity and efficiency.

Furthermore, we examine the unexpected collaboration between rivals Microsoft and Sony in the realm of gaming. The two tech giants announced a partnership to explore cloud gaming and AI solutions together. This collaboration aimed to leverage Microsoft's Azure cloud platform to enhance Sony's PlayStation gaming experience. By joining forces, these competitors were able to pool their resources and expertise to deliver innovative gaming experiences that would otherwise be challenging to achieve individually.

Additionally, we delve into the collaboration between Google and NASA. This unexpected partnership resulted in the creation of Google Earth, a powerful mapping and visualization tool that provided users with a virtual exploration of the planet. By combining Google's mapping technology with NASA's satellite imagery and scientific data, this collaboration offered a groundbreaking way to explore and understand the Earth's landscapes, features, and climate patterns.

Through exploring these unexpected collaborations, we gain insights into the power of cross-industry partnerships and the potential for innovation that emerges when unlikely allies join forces. These collaborations have showcased the ability to combine diverse strengths, expertise, and resources to create groundbreaking solutions that transcend traditional boundaries.

Join us as we unravel the unexpected collaborations and their outcomes in the tech industry. By examining these partnerships, we gain a deeper understanding of the importance of open-mindedness, strategic alignment, and the willingness to embrace unexpected allies. These stories highlight the potential for transformation and the power of collaboration in driving innovation, disrupting industries, and shaping the future of technology.

Chapter 6
Beyond the Boardroom

A. The personal lives and motivations of tech titans

In this chapter, we venture beyond the boardroom and delve into the personal lives and motivations of tech titans, shedding light on the human side of these influential industry game changers. While their professional achievements have shaped the technological landscape, their personal journeys, aspirations, and values provide a deeper understanding of what drives their success.

We explore the early lives and formative experiences of tech titans, uncovering the events and influences that shaped their paths. From humble beginnings to moments of inspiration, we delve into their personal histories to understand the pivotal moments that ignited their passion for technology and innovation. By examining their upbringing, education, and personal struggles, we gain insights into the factors that molded their character and propelled them on their journeys.

Moreover, we explore the motivations and aspirations that drive tech titans in their relentless pursuit of innovation. We delve into their visionary thinking, their desire to make a positive impact on the world, and their commitment to pushing the boundaries of what is possible. We examine how their personal values and beliefs influence their strategic decisions, philanthropic endeavors, and long-term goals.

Additionally, we shine a light on the personal challenges and setbacks that tech titans have faced along their journeys. We explore the resilience, determination, and adaptability that have enabled them to overcome obstacles and persevere in the face of adversity. By examining their personal struggles and the lessons learned from failures, we gain insights into the qualities that have propelled them forward and shaped their leadership styles.

Furthermore, we delve into the philanthropic endeavors and social impact initiatives undertaken by tech titans. We explore their commitments to giving back to society, addressing pressing global challenges, and making a difference beyond their professional pursuits. Whether through charitable foundations, impact investing, or initiatives focused on education and healthcare, we examine how tech titans leverage their resources and influence to effect positive change.

Through exploring the personal lives and motivations of tech titans, we gain a deeper appreciation for the individuals behind the industry giants. Their personal stories humanize their accomplishments and remind us that innovation is driven not only by intellect and business acumen but also by passion, perseverance, and a desire to shape a better future.

Join us as we journey beyond the boardroom and explore the personal lives and motivations of tech titans. By examining their personal journeys, values, and aspirations, we gain insights into the multifaceted nature of their success and the human dimensions that underpin their remarkable achievements. These stories inspire us to look beyond the headlines and recognize the individuals behind the innovations, reminding us that the power to make a difference lies within each of us.

B. Philanthropic endeavors and social responsibility

In this chapter, we delve into the philanthropic endeavors and social responsibility initiatives undertaken by tech titans, exploring their commitment to giving back to society and making a positive impact beyond their boardroom successes. These industry game changers recognize the importance of leveraging their resources, influence, and innovative thinking to address pressing global challenges and contribute to the betterment of society.

We examine the diverse philanthropic initiatives established by tech titans, ranging from charitable foundations to impact investing and social entrepreneurship. We delve into the areas they prioritize, such as education, healthcare, environmental sustainability, and social justice. Through their philanthropic endeavors, these tech titans aim to create positive change, empower communities, and foster long-term, sustainable solutions.

One notable example is the Bill and Melinda Gates Foundation, established by Microsoft co-founder Bill Gates and his wife, Melinda. We explore their philanthropic efforts in combating global health issues, improving education access, and addressing poverty. Their foundation's initiatives, such as the Global Polio Eradication Initiative and the Global Education Program, have had a significant impact on millions of lives worldwide.

Additionally, we delve into the philanthropic initiatives of other tech titans, such as Mark Zuckerberg and Priscilla Chan's Chan Zuckerberg Initiative, which focuses on advancing education, science, and criminal justice reform. We examine the efforts of Salesforce CEO Marc Benioff, who has championed social responsibility through initiatives like the 1-1-1 model, committing 1% of Salesforce's equity, time, and product to philanthropy.

Moreover, we explore the broader concept of social responsibility embraced by tech titans. We examine their efforts to integrate sustainability practices into their operations, reduce environmental footprints, and promote responsible supply chain management. We also explore their commitments to diversity and inclusion, fostering inclusive workplaces and advocating for equitable opportunities within the tech industry.

Through exploring these philanthropic endeavors and social responsibility initiatives, we gain insights into the values and vision that drive tech titans beyond their business pursuits. We examine the transformative potential of their resources and expertise when applied to pressing societal challenges. These efforts highlight their recognition of the importance of corporate citizenship and their dedication to using their positions of influence to effect positive change.

Join us as we explore the philanthropic endeavors and social responsibility initiatives of tech titans. By examining their commitments to social impact, we gain a deeper appreciation for their efforts to create a more equitable, sustainable, and compassionate world. These stories inspire us to consider the power of technology and innovation as tools for social good, and encourage us to think critically about the responsibilities we all have in addressing the pressing challenges of our time.

C. Unveiling the human side behind the industry giants

In this chapter, we go beyond the boardroom to unveil the human side of tech titans, exploring the personal stories, values, and experiences that shape these industry giants. Behind the exceptional success and groundbreaking innovations, these individuals have unique journeys, struggles, and aspirations that contribute to their remarkable achievements.

We delve into the personal backgrounds and early lives of tech titans, uncovering the experiences and influences that have shaped their paths. From childhood curiosities to transformative educational experiences, we explore the formative moments that ignited their passion for technology and paved the way for their entrepreneurial endeavors. By understanding their personal histories, we gain insights into the diverse factors that have shaped their identities and propelled them towards success.

Moreover, we explore the human motivations and values that drive tech titans beyond their professional pursuits. We delve into their visions for a better future, their desires to positively impact society, and their commitments to social responsibility. Whether it's a dedication to environmental sustainability, educational empowerment, or health initiatives, we examine how their personal values align with their philanthropic endeavors, and how they strive to leave a lasting positive legacy.

Additionally, we uncover the personal challenges and setbacks that tech titans have encountered on their journeys. Behind their triumphs lie moments of failure, rejection, and self-doubt. We explore how these individuals faced adversity, overcame obstacles, and learned valuable lessons from their experiences. Their resilience, determination, and ability to embrace failure contribute to their ability to navigate the ever-evolving tech landscape.

Furthermore, we examine the leadership styles and approaches that tech titans bring to their companies and teams. By studying their leadership philosophies, management strategies, and communication styles, we gain insights into how they foster innovation, inspire their teams, and shape company cultures. We explore their abilities to empower others, nurture talent, and drive collective success.

Through unveiling the human side of tech titans, we aim to humanize their remarkable achievements and inspire readers with their stories of perseverance, passion, and purpose. By understanding the individuals behind the industry giants, we gain a deeper appreciation for the human qualities and experiences that underpin their extraordinary success.

Join us as we venture beyond the boardroom to unveil the human side of tech titans. Through their personal stories, values, and journeys, we discover the remarkable individuals driving technological advancements and shaping our world. These stories serve as a reminder that behind the innovation and disruption lies a human spirit fueled by curiosity, ambition, and the desire to make a difference.

Chapter 7
Looking Ahead

A. The future of tech titans and their evolving roles

In this final chapter, we peer into the future and examine the evolving roles of tech titans in an ever-changing technological landscape. As the pace of innovation accelerates and new challenges arise, we explore the potential trajectories of these industry giants and the transformations they may undergo.

We begin by considering the expanding scope of tech titans' influence. With their deep pockets, vast resources, and extensive expertise, they have the potential to extend their reach beyond their core industries. We analyze how they may venture into new domains, such as healthcare, renewable energy, transportation, and space exploration. By leveraging their technological prowess and capabilities, they can drive advancements in these sectors and reshape entire industries.

Moreover, we explore the growing importance of responsible innovation and ethical considerations in the future of tech titans. As technology becomes increasingly intertwined with every aspect of our lives, there is a heightened awareness of the potential risks and unintended consequences. We examine how tech titans may prioritize ethical practices, data privacy, algorithmic transparency, and inclusivity to address these concerns and ensure technology serves the greater good.

Additionally, we delve into the evolving role of tech titans as global leaders and influencers. With their immense reach and impact, they have the ability to shape public opinion, influence policy, and contribute to societal progress. We explore how they may use their influence to address pressing global challenges, advocate for sustainable practices, and champion social justice causes. The evolving roles of tech titans as responsible corporate citizens and thought leaders will play a vital role in shaping the future of technology and its impact on society.

Furthermore, we examine the potential for collaboration and cooperation among tech titans to address complex global issues. In a rapidly interconnected world, the challenges we face require collective action and shared resources. We explore how tech titans may come together to tackle issues such as climate change, healthcare disparities, and equitable access to technology. By pooling their expertise and resources, they can leverage collective intelligence to find innovative solutions to these complex challenges.

Through looking ahead, we recognize the uncertainties and disruptions that lie on the horizon. The future of tech titans will be shaped by breakthrough technologies, shifting market dynamics, regulatory landscapes, and evolving consumer expectations. By anticipating these changes and embracing agility, adaptability, and a commitment to continuous innovation, tech titans can navigate the future with resilience and maintain their positions at the forefront of the industry.

Join us as we peer into the future and explore the evolving roles of tech titans. By examining their potential trajectories, ethical considerations, societal impact, and collaborative possibilities, we gain insights into the forces that will shape the tech landscape in the coming years.

The future holds immense possibilities, and the actions and decisions of tech titans will play a pivotal role in defining the next era of technological advancements and their impact on our world.

B. Predictions and speculations about upcoming innovations

In this final chapter, we embark on a journey of speculation and exploration as we make predictions about the upcoming innovations that may shape the future. The tech landscape is ever-evolving, and we examine the emerging trends, technologies, and possibilities that could redefine industries, transform our lives, and propel tech titans to new heights.

One area of speculation lies in the field of artificial intelligence (AI) and machine learning. We anticipate significant advancements in AI algorithms and models, leading to more sophisticated automation, predictive analytics, and personalized experiences. With AI permeating various sectors, from healthcare and finance to transportation and entertainment, we predict that tech titans will continue to invest heavily in AI research and development to unlock its full potential.

Furthermore, we delve into the realm of augmented reality (AR) and virtual reality (VR), envisioning immersive experiences that seamlessly blend the digital and physical worlds. We speculate on the possibilities of AR glasses, VR simulations for training and entertainment, and the integration of these technologies into everyday life. Tech titans may pioneer breakthroughs in AR and VR, creating new avenues for communication, collaboration, and entertainment.

Additionally, we explore the potential of blockchain technology beyond cryptocurrencies. We anticipate its wider adoption in sectors such as supply chain management, digital identity verification, and secure data storage. As tech titans continue to explore the transformative power of blockchain, we predict that they will invest in creating scalable and efficient blockchain solutions, unlocking new levels of transparency, security, and trust.

Moreover, we speculate on the future of transportation, foreseeing advancements in electric and autonomous vehicles. Tech titans are already investing heavily in electric vehicle technology, and we predict that they will continue to push the boundaries of innovation, making electric vehicles more accessible, affordable, and sustainable. We also anticipate advancements in autonomous driving technology, with the potential for widespread adoption of self-driving cars, revolutionizing transportation systems and mobility as we know them.

Additionally, we explore the potential of quantum computing to transform the way we process information. Quantum computing has the potential to solve complex problems exponentially faster than traditional computing systems. We speculate on the possibilities of breakthroughs in quantum computing algorithms, quantum cryptography, and optimization, which could revolutionize fields such as drug discovery, weather forecasting, and financial modeling.

Through these predictions and speculations, we glimpse into the exciting possibilities that lie ahead. The future holds immense potential for technological advancements that will reshape industries, redefine human experiences, and challenge our perception of what is possible. Tech titans, with their vast resources, research capabilities, and entrepreneurial spirit, are at the forefront of driving these innovations and pioneering the technologies that will shape our future.

Join us as we delve into the realm of predictions and speculations about upcoming innovations. By exploring these possibilities, we gain insights into the ever-evolving nature of the tech industry and the potential breakthroughs that await us. The future is ripe with opportunities, and the innovative spirit of tech titans will continue to push the boundaries of what is imaginable, fueling a future where technology plays an even more central role in shaping our world.

C. Reflections on the enduring legacies of these industry game changers

In this final chapter, we reflect on the enduring legacies of tech titans and their profound impact on the world. These industry game changers have left indelible marks on society, transforming the way we live, work, and connect with one another. We explore the lasting contributions they have made and the legacies that will continue to shape the future.

We begin by reflecting on the transformative power of innovation. Tech titans have revolutionized industries, disrupted traditional models, and introduced groundbreaking technologies that have become an integral part of our lives. From smartphones and social media to cloud computing and e-commerce, their innovations have reshaped how we communicate, access information, conduct business, and navigate the digital landscape.

Furthermore, we examine the influence of tech titans on entrepreneurship and startup culture. By paving the way with their own success stories, these industry giants have inspired countless entrepreneurs to pursue their visions and disrupt established norms. They have cultivated a culture of innovation, risk-taking, and exponential growth, encouraging a new generation of innovators to push boundaries and create meaningful change.

Additionally, we reflect on the societal impact of tech titans' philanthropic endeavors. Through their charitable foundations and social responsibility initiatives, they have directed their resources and expertise towards addressing critical global challenges. Their contributions in areas such as education, healthcare, and environmental sustainability have made a tangible difference in the lives of individuals and communities worldwide, leaving a legacy of social impact and positive change.

Moreover, we contemplate the influence of tech titans as thought leaders and influencers. Their visionary thinking, strategic insights, and ability to anticipate trends have shaped the direction of the tech industry and influenced broader societal conversations. From advocating for privacy rights and ethical practices to addressing the ethical implications of emerging technologies, their voices have sparked important dialogues and paved the way for responsible innovation.

We also reflect on the importance of diversity and inclusion in the tech industry, acknowledging the strides made by tech titans in promoting equitable representation and fostering inclusive workplaces. Their efforts to cultivate diverse talent, address gender and racial disparities, and create inclusive environments have set important precedents for the industry and have the potential to inspire a more diverse and inclusive future.

Through reflecting on the enduring legacies of tech titans, we recognize the profound and far-reaching impact they have had on our world. Their contributions have transcended business success and have influenced the very fabric of our society. Their legacies serve as a reminder of the power of human ingenuity, the possibilities of technology, and the potential for individuals to shape the world around them.

Join us as we reflect on the enduring legacies of tech titans. By recognizing their contributions, we gain a deeper appreciation for the transformative power of innovation, the importance of social responsibility, and the possibilities that lie ahead. These industry game changers have left a lasting imprint on our collective consciousness, and their legacies will continue to shape the future as we navigate the ever-evolving landscape of technology and its profound impact on society.

Conclusion

A. Summarizing the untold stories and their significance

As we come to the end of this journey exploring the untold stories of tech titans, we reflect on the significance of these narratives and the profound impact they have had on the world. Throughout the chapters, we have uncovered the personal journeys, visionary thinking, and groundbreaking innovations that have propelled these industry game changers to their positions of influence. The untold stories of tech titans not only shed light on their individual successes but also reveal broader themes and lessons that shape our understanding of the technological landscape and its societal implications.

We began by recognizing the importance of technology in shaping our world, establishing the context for the rise of tech titans as influential industry game changers. We explored their humble beginnings, visionary ideas, and the relentless pursuit of innovation that set them apart. From the early pioneers to the disruptive technologies they introduced, we gained insights into the transformative power of their contributions.

As we ventured further, we uncovered the challenges, strategies, and unexpected collaborations that shaped the journeys of tech titans. We explored their impact on traditional industries, their ethical dilemmas, and the societal implications of their practices. We recognized their philanthropic endeavors and social responsibilities, highlighting their commitment to making a positive impact beyond their boardroom successes. Through these stories, we gained a deeper appreciation for the multifaceted nature of their achievements and the complex dynamics that surround their roles as industry leaders.

Looking ahead, we speculated on the future of tech titans and the innovations that may shape the technological landscape. We envisioned the potential of emerging technologies, the evolving roles of tech titans as global influencers, and the importance of responsible innovation in driving positive change. These speculations remind us of the ever-evolving nature of the tech industry and the immense possibilities that lie on the horizon.

In conclusion, the untold stories of tech titans unveil the human side, motivations, and legacies behind the industry giants. They inspire us to embrace innovation, push boundaries, and strive for positive societal impact. These stories remind us that the world of technology is not just about products, services, and profits; it is about the people driving change, their values, and their dedication to shaping a better future.

As we close this book, we invite you to reflect on the untold stories and the enduring legacies of tech titans. May their journeys inspire you to embrace your own potential, think critically about the role of technology in our lives, and consider the responsibilities we all have in shaping a future where innovation, ethics, and social impact go hand in hand. The untold stories of tech titans are a testament to the power of human ingenuity, and their impact will continue to reverberate in the ever-evolving world of technology.

B. Final thoughts on the impact of tech titans

As we conclude this exploration of the untold stories of tech titans, we are left with profound reflections on their lasting impact. The influence of these industry game changers extends far beyond their companies and the technology they create. Their impact has reshaped industries, transformed societies, and fundamentally altered the way we live our lives.

Tech titans have not only revolutionized how we communicate, access information, and conduct business, but they have also become cultural icons, symbols of innovation, and embodiments of the possibilities that lie within the realm of technology. They have disrupted traditional models, challenged established norms, and pushed the boundaries of what is imaginable.

The impact of tech titans is seen in the ways they have empowered individuals and communities. Through their innovations, they have democratized access to information, creating a more connected and globally aware society. They have opened doors for entrepreneurs, enabling a new wave of startups and driving economic growth. By driving technological advancements, they have improved efficiency, enhanced productivity, and created new opportunities for collaboration and creativity.

However, it is essential to acknowledge that their impact is not without challenges and controversies. As tech titans have amassed immense power and influence, questions of privacy, data security, and ethical practices have arisen. The unprecedented scale and reach of their platforms have raised concerns about monopolistic tendencies, algorithmic biases, and the potential for undue influence. It is crucial for tech titans to navigate these challenges with a sense of responsibility, transparency, and accountability.

Looking ahead, the impact of tech titans will continue to shape our future. The pace of innovation shows no signs of slowing down, and as new technologies emerge, the role of tech titans in driving progress and addressing societal challenges becomes increasingly important. They have the power to tackle complex issues such as climate change, healthcare access, and equitable technological advancements.

It is our collective responsibility to ensure that the impact of tech titans remains positive and inclusive. The relationship between technology and society is symbiotic, and as consumers, policymakers, and individuals, we have a role to play in shaping the future. We must foster a culture of responsible innovation, one that upholds ethical standards, respects user privacy, and values diversity and inclusion.

In conclusion, the untold stories of tech titans reveal the profound impact they have had on our world. Their contributions have been transformative, sparking societal changes, fueling economic growth, and inspiring the next generation of innovators. As we move forward, let us embrace the possibilities of technology while also recognizing the need for thoughtful reflection, ethical considerations, and collaboration to ensure that the impact of tech titans continues to drive positive change and create a future that benefits all.

C. Encouraging further exploration and discussion

As we reach the conclusion of this captivating journey through the untold stories of tech titans, we invite you to continue exploring, discussing, and contemplating the fascinating world of technology and its impact on our lives. The stories shared within this book have merely scratched the surface of the vast tapestry that encompasses the accomplishments, challenges, and legacies of these industry game changers.

We encourage you to delve deeper into the lives and contributions of tech titans, as there is always more to uncover and learn. From biographies and memoirs to documentaries and interviews, there are numerous resources available that offer unique perspectives and insights. By delving into these additional materials, you can gain a more comprehensive understanding of the individuals behind the innovations and the contexts in which they operate.

Furthermore, we invite you to engage in discussions and debates surrounding the impact of tech titans and the broader implications of technology in our society. Technology is a complex and multifaceted realm, and by engaging in thoughtful conversations, we can collectively shape the narrative, share diverse perspectives, and explore the potential risks and opportunities that lie ahead.

Consider joining or forming communities that foster dialogue on technology, innovation, and its impact. Participate in conferences, seminars, and online forums where experts and enthusiasts gather to discuss the latest trends, advancements, and ethical considerations. Through collaboration and knowledge sharing, we can collectively navigate the challenges and seize the opportunities presented by the rapidly evolving tech landscape.

Additionally, we encourage you to stay informed about the latest developments in the tech industry. Subscribe to reputable publications, follow thought leaders, and engage with industry news to remain abreast of the ever-changing landscape. By staying informed, you can actively participate in shaping the future of technology and contribute to the ongoing discourse surrounding its impact on our lives.

Lastly, take the insights gained from the untold stories of tech titans and apply them to your own pursuits and endeavors. Embrace innovation, think critically about the potential impact of your ideas, and strive for ethical and responsible practices. Whether you are an aspiring entrepreneur, a student, or simply an enthusiast, the lessons and inspiration derived from the tech titans can serve as a guiding force in your own journey.

In conclusion, the untold stories of tech titans serve as a reminder of the power of human ingenuity, perseverance, and innovation. By exploring their narratives, engaging in discussions, and staying curious, we can actively contribute to shaping the future of technology and its impact on our world. Let us continue to explore, learn, and collaborate as we navigate the ever-evolving landscape of technology together.

www.ingramcontent.com/pod-product-compliance
Lightning Source LLC
LaVergne TN
LVHW051716050326
832903LV00032B/4244